The 7 Secrets Of Gain~~~~~~~
More Sales & Greater Profits

WHY FACTS
TELL
BUT STORIES
SELL

by
BILL GOSS

Published by

www.elitepublishingacademy.com

First Edition published 2020
© Bill Goss
Printed and bound in Great Britain by
www.elitepublishingacademy.com

A catalogue record for this book
is available from The British Library
ISBN 978-1-912713-91-2

Dedication

To everyone who has tried and failed and tried again. This book is for every one of you.

Everybody has a story to tell that can help others. If you believe in your own truths and choose not to hide them away, I can assure you that you will be blown away by the response you will receive. And you will never fail again.

To my two amazing children Ava & Jack.

Always believe in what you can achieve, there is nothing stopping you.

"Whatever the mind can conceive and believe, the mind can achieve" - Napoleon Hill.

Nothing changes if you stay comfortable.

Let's go chase the sun.

Live, Laugh and Love xx

Bill Goss

Bill Goss
Founder, Elite Publishing Academy

CONTENTS

Introduction

By picking up this book, you have taken the first step in mastering a very different way of marketing your business.

What you will read over the course of this book will teach you how to significantly grow your business - simply by being you.

You are here for one reason and one reason only: to grow your business and take it to a higher level; quickly, easily and with far less work than you might imagine.

That's it.

That's why I've written this book, and that's what it's designed to help you do.

If you put into practice even a fraction of what you discover in these pages, you'll be head and shoulders above your competitors.

And if you're one of the 20% who do 80% of what's contained in this book, you'll be well on your way to the kind of business and life most people only ever dream of.

All opinions expressed in this book are mine and mine alone. This is a labour of love and I really want to share my experience with you to help you achieve exactly what you want to achieve. So let's get going...

CHAPTER ONE

COMMUNICATING IN THE AGE OF NOISE

The world we live in has never been noisier.

Never has it been easier to communicate with people, to reach potential new customers in any part of the world, day and night, right around the clock.

And yet ironically, never has it been harder to make our voices heard above the noise of everybody shouting at once, night and day, 24/7 and 365.

As a businessman or woman, communication is key to your business' success.

You may create the greatest product or offer the most amazing service known to mankind, but if you are unable to communicate the benefits of that product or service to the people who would buy or use it, then you have ultimately failed - or at very least fallen short of reaching that product's potential.

Because, as a very clever thinker once noted, 'If a tree falls in a forest and no one is around to hear it, does it make a sound?' Your business may not be a tree but it's not really any different.

Like it or not - some people do and some people don't - marketing your business and making it attractive to potential clients and customers relies on storytelling.

To succeed in that, you have to be a storyteller.

Now, in its most basic form, telling the world who you are is storytelling.

Your business' website, your email marketing, the newsletters you write, the advertising you do, the Tweets or Insta snapshots you send out every now and then... whatever medium you choose, you have to tell the world who you are for them to be aware that you exist.

You have to make some noise, but you have to make that noise wisely. Because if you become known as a person who makes noise but says nothing, people will switch off and leave you well alone. So you have to master the Art of Noise. Which sounds hard but really it isn't.

We live in a world of instant gratification, where the need for speed is everywhere and in everything. Few potential clients or customers have the time to wait for you to ramble on before getting to the point. They want what they want now, if not sooner, and they don't have the time to wait.

The great Swedish power balladeers Roxette nailed this one with their greatest hits compilation. Titled: Don't Bore Us, Get To The Chorus, it probably wasn't referring to marketing your business but it definitely could have been. Because Roxette identified that everyone wants everything now, if not sooner. That's why your story - your message - has to be quick, sharp and bang on the money. Because if you can't get to the chorus fast, your clients will bugger off to someone who can.

But telling the world who you are is just the start, the most basic of basics.

Just telling the world who you are is not enough. Not even close.

Whoever you are and whatever you do, you absolutely have to tell your potential customers or clients what you do and - every bit as crucially - how it will benefit them. How will it make them better at what they do? How will it save them money or make them richer? How will it help their own business run more efficiently or more effectively, or preferably both? Ultimately, how will they be happier and more prosperous as a result of using your services? In other words, and in no uncertain terms, they will be asking themselves: What's in it for me? And rightly so.

You need to have the answer and to deliver it quickly and effectively.

Let's consider your website here as a good example of cutting through noise.

Now, we're assuming you have a website, a platform that allows you to market your business to the whole entire world and possibly beyond. If you don't have one, write out one hundred times "I am a fecking fool who needs to get myself a website now." Because you are and you do - and you shouldn't need telling that.

A business that would happily sell its wares to the nation, the world and quite possibly beyond but has no online presence is delivering what the kids once called (but possibly don't any more) and epic fail.

Having no website is like opening your mouth to shout about your business and no noise coming out; just a pathetic shrill nothing. You're impotent and your business won't be heard above those who are taking it seriously with proper, functional, high-achieving websites. You need one of those and you need it fast. But before you look into getting one, let me tell you something you really do need to know.

A slick, sleek, all-the-bells-and-whistles website built by some fancy, expensive, tech internet setup isn't what you need. It isn't what your business needs. At least, not necessarily. The one key thing your business needs is a message - a clear message that conveys (a) what you are, (b) what you do and (c), and crucially, how what you do can benefit your ideal client. That message needs to be very quickly established, before they get bored and bugger off.

If you have a highly polished website that does that for you, that's great and it will be money and time well spent. But if you have a highly polished website that fails to convey (a), (b) and (c) clearly and quickly, then it's time and money pissed down the drain.

If your message and your call to action - buy this product from me now, essentially - is buried away on page 7, behind pages on how your business got started, behind page after page of dull and unnecessary bios of your staff and behind photos and graphics that look very sleek but which don't serve any purpose, your website is failing.

In this day and age, you can build a very basic website for relatively little financial outlay and it can feature very few pages and absolutely no imagery whatsoever. It might not win an award for how it looks, but that does not matter. If it functions properly then you are winning.

And by 'function properly' we refer again to that (a), (b) and (c). Your website absolutely has to tell a prospective client what you are and what you do, although the fact they are on your website in the first place suggests they probably know that much already. But what it must do quickly, efficiently and very, very effectively is tell that client how whatever it is that you do will benefit them.

Why? Because people are selfish.

At this point, that client doesn't care at all about you. They do not care that you can ride a unicycle, you have a Cockapoo named Dr Dre or that you once won a hotdog eating contest - although 27 in three minutes is nothing to be sniffed at.

At this moment in time, that potential client does not give two hoots about any of that. All they care about is what's in it for them. And so they should. They only care about what your business or your product or service can do for them, and the clear and very obvious ways it will benefit their life.

They are sitting there in front of you with money in their pocket. By just being there they have shown that they are willing to buy from you - they just need you to convince them that what you are selling is worth them buying. They need to be convinced that they will benefit - What's In It For Me? Or WIIFM, as we shall from this point forth refer to it.

Filling your palm with money

Now, how your website goes about turning an inter-ested but cautious visitor into a slaveringly keen client who wants to fill your palm with money is a much bigger subject, one for another book or conversation 9hey, we can talk - call the number at the end of the book or visit our very effective website now).

For now, all you need to really know is that your web-site messaging needs to be clear and clever. It has to move your potential client from the start to the finish quickly and efficiently, without them losing interest and going somewhere else.

If your website is cluttered with superfluous waffle and if it offers no clear route from arriving to purchasing your services, then it is failing and you'll need to address the problem fast.

If it fails to tell your potential client about the benefits to them, instead focussing on the company history or the fact your office is beside a lovely river, then it is failing you and you'll need to address the problem fast.

And if it talks far more about you than about them, then it has failed and you need to etc and so on.

On that final point, here's a quick game. If you already have a website, look on your homepage and count up the number of times the word 'we', 'our' or 'I' appears.

Now, count up the number of times the words 'you', 'your' or 'yours' appears in that same copy. As a general rule, you should have three times as many 'yous' and 'yours' as 'Us' and 'ours'. Because this is only partly about you but mainly about them - how they can benefit. So you absolutely have to write about your customer and you absolutely have to get it right. Which is easier said than done, but here's some advice that will make it easier.

To understand your client, you need to understand who they are, what makes them whistle and why they are interested in whatever service you are looking to provide them with. To do that, you have to truly understand what makes them tick as a businessman or woman - because ultimately, people do business with people, not with businesses, so it all comes down to human emotions - hopes, fears and expectations. (This is why building your list is so vital, because the people on your list are already familiar with you, with what you do, what you offer, how you can be of help. But we'll come onto that later on.)

Now, most businesses out there rely on hope marketing. They create a product, put it out there via their website or wherever else and they hope. They simply sit back and hope the customers are drawn to it, like moths to flames and flies on... well, yeah, you get the picture.

That kind of marketing is a complete waste of time and money. A few customers may wander in and a few of them may even make a purchase, but it's entirely luck rather than judgement and the numbers are so much lower than they would be if they only understood their customer.

So you need to build your ideal client's avatar - his or her profile, in as much detail as possible. To do this the easy way, grab a pen and paper and answer the following questions.

1. Who is my customer, or ideally, my client?
2. What do they need that I provide?
3. If there's something I offer that they do not purchase, what is stopping them?
4. What do they need that I don't currently provide?
5. Could I provide that thing that they also need?
6. What keeps them awake at night?
7. What can I do to build a stronger relationship with them, to take away the sleepless nights and the worry and the stress?

Of course, if you want to be able to paint a more accurate picture of your client, ask them directly. Again - this is where your list will come in so very handily. Ask your existing clients what they need to enable their business to perform more effectively for them.

Ask them why they use you, what they think you do well, what they think you could do better and what you don't do that perhaps you could. Note it all down, thank them for their insight, then set about responding to what they've just told you.

The problem a lot of businesses have is not truly knowing their client, so they have no hope of being able to speak to them, to answer their needs effectively. They think that their customer is like them, that they share the same needs. And while there may be some crossover, this is largely not true. You are not your customer. Full stop.

And until you understand who your customer truly is, you will be falling short.

Don't let them fly away It's only once you've defined your customer and built your avatar that you can start to move beyond hope marketing and into a more effective, accurate way of selling your business. It's only now that you can think about your messaging and making sure that what you tell the world is what they actually want. Which brings us back to your website - remember that? It could just as easily be your landing page or any other platform you use for marketing, the same rules will apply, but let's focus on your website.

As we've established, your website absolutely has to have a very clear, demonstrable benefit to your customer or client's business and/or to them as an individual. It needs to be far less about you and far more about them. If it doesn't, then why would they bother?

They are busy people and they've already switched off - they've gone in search of someone who knows how to sell their product and its benefits far more effectively than you - they've gone to someone who understands them more than you do.

But they won't fly away if you've built your avatar effectively. Because if you've defined clearly who they are and what they need from you, you're able and equipped to speak to them more directly. Get that bit right and you can better define what you do and most crucially, how it can improve their business and their life as a result of them buying it from you.

It's a simple process, but it's more complicated than so many businesses realise, which is good news for you. Because by understanding how your marketing should work, you'll be able to make your voice heard above all the other noise - the noisy hawkers hoping that if they make enough noise, someone might listen to them. The hope marketers who are effectively winging it, although not very effectively.

The Age of Noise

The fact that every herbert and his dog are making noise is bad news on the one hand, because it does make it hard to be heard, for your message to be noticed and acted upon. However, the fact that most small businesses are very poor at marketing themselves is very good news.

Many businesses - perhaps including many of your competitors - make a lot of noise, but they are not making quality noise. They do not understand how to focus that noise, to harness it so that it's not just noise. They just bang on. And on. And on. And hope and hope and hope. And mainly, it serves no purpose and has no positive effect.

But by understanding a few basic but fundamental laws of marketing, you can become very good at marketing and learn how to make the right noise at the right time. Combine those few fundamentals with knowing your clients and knowing exactly what they want to make their lives better and you'll have a very powerful combination, one that will make you far more effective in business.

Now, learning the marketing basics isn't difficult or particularly time-consuming, anyone can learn it fast and without it making their brain hurt. Becoming a highly-skilled marketing type does take more time and energy than you'd probably want to put in, but even learning a few basics will help elevate you above so many other businesses who waste their time and money making the wrong type of noise.

So let's start with a very basic lesson - perhaps even a refresher for many readers: Understanding The Marketing Funnel - how a business goes about attracting and retaining its customers.

Anyone in business knows the importance of marketing and of moving people through the marketing funnel, generally through six stages. And if they don't know it, they really, definitely and absolutely should, so let's recap...

- **Step 1. Unaware**
- **Step 2. Aware**
- **Step 3. Interested**
- **Step 4. Customer**
- **Step 5. Repeat Customer**
- **Step 6. Advocate**

At the outset, everyone is **Unaware** of your product or service. Nobody knows about it, bar the people working on it and your nearest and dearest.

To make everyone else Aware, you have to tick off all the classic marketing options: The website, the email marketing, the local or national advertising campaign, the Tweets and Instagram and everything else you can do to spread the word.

At that point they become **Aware**, but moving a person from Aware to the ultimate end goal of flag-waving, tub-thumping Advocate takes time and no little persuasion. It's definitely worth the effort.

Once they're Aware, hopefully then they're **Interested** in what you do - interested enough to become a Customer. If they become a **Customer**, you then want them to be so happy with your product or service that they become a **Repeat Customer**, at which point momentum is in your favour.

Repeat Customers who are particularly happy with a service or product often become the most valuable customer of all: **The Advocate**.

Far fewer in number than those people further up the funnel, the Advocate is incredibly valuable and will do much of your marketing for you. They will recommend you to others, and if those others also like what you're doing and the service you provide, they too will become Advocates and the process will continue.

Now, reaching the Unaware has never been easier, thanks largely to the advent of the Internet and the powers of social media in its many guises. Reaching a vast audience is the easy part. Being heard by them is far tougher, because of all that aforementioned noise and their increasing impatience. Getting them to pay attention and listen to you over everyone else is tricky.

However...

There are a number of ways to make your voice heard and your words stick, the most important being to understand who you are marketing to. You have to understand your customer or would-be customer, the type of person you are trying to appeal to.

You may think you know exactly who that customer is, but it never ever hurts to define who they are. To do this, you really should engage in a little SWOT analysis. To do this, grab a notepad and a pen, if you're old school, or open your LapBook Pro X if you're fully 2020, and note down the letter 'S' - the first letter of SWOT.

▣ **S** is for Strengths.

Note down your strengths - yours personally in a business sense and your business strengths. What are you particularly good at? What do you do really well, what do you do that elevates you above other similar businesses? Why do you customers choose you above the alternatives?

▣ **W** is for Weaknesses.

This time, note down the areas where you think you could improve, the things you think you don't do so well, anything you think you should stop doing completely. Be honest and don't be afraid to be brutal, it will help you grow as a business and as a person.

▣ **O** is for Opportunities.

As the Pet Shop Boys noted, there are lots of opportunities and if there aren't you can make them. Look at your industry and ask yourself are there any gaps you could move into. Is there a new product or service you could provide that would fill that gap? Look at the emerging trends in your industry and ask yourself how you can get ahead of them. Getting ahead is always very good, so take the time to study where your market is and where it looks to be going.

▣ **T** is for Threats.

Finally, write down the threats to your business, the main challenges you face, the things that could have a negative impact on what you do. This could be the onset of expensive and/or confusing technology. It could be

cash flow, it could be managing bad or problematic customers. In fact it can be anything that could damage your
business. Address the issues early and you're in a much
better position to deal with them.

The reason to undergo a SWOT analysis of your own
business is to get a better understanding of what you do
- what you do well and the things that attract customers
to you, and what you could improve to hopefully attract
more business.

If you don't understand what makes you and your business unique, you can't possibly hope to sell yourself to
clients quickly or effectively.

As an example of this, consider your website for a moment. Front and centre on the homepage or landing page,
you have to establish very clearly what you do and - as
mentioned before - how what you do will benefit the person reading the words.

The person reading is probably busy, likely impatient
and understandably selfish and if you can't sum up what
you do and the benefit to customers in an instant, they will
go elsewhere and you will have lost a potential customer
and possibly a long term client.

So you have to understand what makes your business
special and attractive to potential customers, and you
have to be able to define it in any marketing you do. That's
why the SWOT analysis is key.

If you're struggling to really nail down what makes your business unique, you could always ask your long term clients what you do so well that makes them buy from you rather than your rivals - because they know better than anybody. An alternative option is to take three pieces of paper and write down the three reasons you think your customers buy from you, one reason on each piece.

Consider the three reasons you've written for a moment, then discard the weakest of them - throw it in the bin. Now consider the two reasons you're left with and discard the weakest of the two - bin it. What you're left with is the single, most important reason people buy from you - and now you have that reason you can use that information to better understand your customers, but equally, understand what it is you do. Which brings us back to the six-step marketing funnel.

Now, if you can define who you are quickly and effectively to attract the Unaware and make them Aware of your business, you can move more effectively through those six stages. Once they're Aware of you, you can work on fast-tracking them first to Interested and then on to Customer. One very effective easy of doing this - arguably _**the most effective way**_, in fact - is by proving your authority.

Establishing your authority is absolutely key and it's easier than you may think - particularly if you use an essential short-cut. Now this is so important, it deserves a sub-heading all of its own...

The Art & Effectiveness Of Authority Marketing

Authority marketing is - as the name suggests - the concept of marketing from authority. This means being positioned as an expert in your field, so that any claims you make come from a position of authority. When your arguments come from a position of authority, people are much more inclined to listen. As an authority, you have a higher level of trust and significantly more clout. Your voice becomes louder and you'll find it can carry further.

Consider the following, very simple scenario. If you were being offered advice by two people and one of them was considered to be an authority or an expert on the subject, while the other was just another man or woman in the street, who would you be more inclined to listen to? If both of them had equally compelling arguments, and both delivered with the same effectiveness, the argument from the authority figure would always win out.

This is the same concept as testimonials and social proof - the psychological phenomenon where people assume the actions of influencers in certain scenarios.

If you're considering using a person or a company for a product or a service, it's highly likely that before making a call to them you will look to see who they've worked with previously and how they are reviewed and rated by those customers. You do it to others and don't doubt for a second that they will be doing it with you. It's simply doing your due diligence.

Such practices are entirely understandable and are the lifeblood of the B2B sales industry. It's very hard to get by without being able to prove your credentials. Think about it. If two plumbers turn up at your door to fix your leaking toilet, are you trusting the one who arrived on foot with his tools in a carrier bag, or the man with his qualifications plastered large across across the side of his van? They may do an equal job but we trust those who can prove their authority, because we seek a guarantee that we can trust the person we do business with, to reduce the element of risk.

So how do you establish your authority? Put simply, the more social proof you have, the easier it becomes to stand out from the crowd and to ensure your voice is heard above the noise. "Everybody wants what everybody wants, nobody wants what nobody wants", as the noted US businesswoman Barbara Corcoran. And while that's a statement you can file in a box marked 'Bleedin' Obvious', it happens to be true.

The marketing sensation Neil Patel is an excellent example of the power of testimonials and social proof. If you're a large enterprise and you're looking to hire the best marketer you possibly can, who are you going to listen to? A generic marketing agency? Or the guy endorsed by Forbes, President Obama and the United Nations? No need to answer that, it's entirely rhetorical and can also be filed in that box of the Bleedin' Obvious.

But Neil Patel didn't suddenly arrive as an authority. He had to work his way up to that position, step by step over a number of years. He had to prove his authority so that people trusted what he told them. He did that in a number of highly effective ways, which we'll touch upon more in the following chapter. Suffice to say that what he does and what you do may be poles apart, but many of the same practices drive him that drive you - or at least they should do. It's all about gaining an advantage over your competition, and this is a subject significant enough to also warrant a new sub-heading...

How to Gain An Unfair Advantage

So much of marketing effectively is about staying ahead of the competition. If you can elevate yourself above your competitors and make your message heard above their noise, you're in a far stronger position.

The problem is, if all your competitors who do a similar job and offer a similar service all have excellent testimonials and similarly solid case studies, how do you differentiate and elevate yourself above them? And make no mistake, you have to be 'different', because if you're just doing what everyone else is doing, you're likely to fall pack into the pack - and you don't want to be back in the pack when you should be standing out.

This brings us on to the Three Ps - the thing that so often comes into the equation when people are considering buying a product or service. This is they...

1. **Product**
2. **Price**
3. **Perceived Value**

OK, you pedant, we'll call it the 'Three Ps and a V'.

Product and Price need little explanation. If the customer wants or needs something you can provide and they like the price it's being offered at, there's a good chance you'll do business.

The third option is more complex, however. Perceived Value is how much someone thinks you or your product are worth, based on their evaluation of its quality or desirability compared to its peers. This is where you really need to stand out, rather than be just another business in a long line of businesses.

Here's an example of Perceived Value. Are Apple's iPhones worth the very high prices people pay for them? If you broke the cost of each phone down into the components contained within each case, you could easily argue not. Break down those components and you might find they are similar in cost to products used on any other mobile phone, yet the product is priced significantly higher. Why?

Well, it's largely because Apple is perceived as the authority as far as smart phones are concerned by much of the general public, so people willingly pay a premium price for their products and their brand. They trust Apple to sell them the very best product that money can buy. And Apple are by no means alone in this. Nike, Dyson, Coca-Cola,

Sony and many other brands you probably have in your house right now also enjoy that very elevated position. Each of them ticks the Perceived Value box.

You may never become an Apple or a Nike. You may never breathe the same rarefied air as brands of that size and you may never actually want to. But Perceived Value also affects you and your business - because it affects every business.

Has there ever been a time when you've lost out on a piece of work that you were perfect for. Perhaps you lost out to a bigger, better known competitor, even though you know you'd have done every bit as good a job...

If you have, you'll no doubt wish there was a way that you could level the playing field and stack the odds a little more in your favour. The good news is that there is.

It starts by building a reputation that helps establish that much sought after Perceived Value. But that's a story for another chapter...

CHAPTER TWO

BECOME THE AUTHORITY

> ### *Authority*
> noun: The power or right to give orders, make decisions, and enforce obedience.

To become trusted, you have to establish authority in your area of expertise.

To be an authority is to be an expert on a subject. And as much as you may consider yourself an authority, you must convince others of that for it to be effective. That stands to reason, right.

Authority is generated in one of three ways.

1. Implied authority
2. Authority from social proof
3. Authority from thought leadership

Let's take these in order.

1. Implied authority

A very good example of implied authority is a uniform. If we see a police officer on duty it is immediately implied that they have authority. They are in charge of enforcing the law - their uniform implies their authority, their training and their position. A doctor's white coat is another good example.

A doctor doesn't need to publish a book for us to know he's an expert in his field - his white coat says it all. It tells you that this person spent years in education and has earned the uniform. Robert Cialdini writes about the concept of implied authority in his book Influence: The Psychology of Persuasion, which is well worth a read if you'd like to know more on this topic.

2. Authority from social proof

This is where testimonials and case studies come in, and why they are so important. Social proof tells others you've done something well before and you can do it again. It's a trust signal that lowers the risk factor as far as the decision-making process goes. If you are trusted by others as an authority, it's much easier for me to view you as an authority. A company that has mastered social proof is Shopify. They have cornered the market as far as do-it-yourself small online stores go. Are there better solutions out there? Sure, WooCommerce to name just one.

But Shopify basically came out of nowhere and captured a huge chunk of the market with their incredibly customer success-focused marketing. They have a huge number of success stories across basically every vertical and write loads of well researched, long form content on how to bootstrap and grow shops from scratch, referencing their own customers who have done the same on their platform - establishing authority from social proof.

Another good example of this is Amazon, the online superstore rather than the rainforest. Think about every time you go on their website to buy something new, something you haven't purchased before. If it's ever, in any way a risk purchase - i.e. something you may have any level of uncertainty about - you'll almost certainly check out the reviews and ratings before you hit 'Purchase'. And if it comes down to two products that look and are priced roughly the same, the chances are you'll opt for the one with a higher overall rating and a higher number of ratings. You're doing what every sane purchaser ever does - taking the risk out of the purchase by using social proof to steer your decision. So as you can see, social proof is incredibly powerful.

3. Authority from thought leadership

You could also call this the 'proof is in the pudding approach'. Authority from thought leadership is gained by doing - by demonstrating you know what you're talking about and by giving away free value to others. This is the whole point behind blogging and vlogging. Nobody knows what you know, until you tell them what you know. Creating useful, informative content and either giving it away or selling it to others demonstrates first-hand exactly how much you know. To be a thought leader, you have to prove it.

Building thought leadership is not a new concept. It's been around since the dawn of time, in one form or another. Politicians, business people, academics, trades people, friends at the local bar, we all practice thought leadership by presenting compelling arguments. Whether it's convincing a friend or colleague that a particular car or brand of beer is the better way to go, or recommending a book that particularly inspired you, we all engage in thought leadership of one kind or another.

True thought leadership is earned by giving value and 'selling' that value through effective communication - through the storytelling we mentioned earlier. At a certain point, after giving away 'X' amount of value, and as long as what you give away is deemed to be of sufficient value to others, you will automatically become an authority. Sadly, you won't get a badge or a certificate that confirms you are now an authority. Nor is it possible to say when you'll ascend to the position of trusted authority. You might find you become a trusted authority and pick up leads or sales from a single video tutorial you post online, or it might take months and months of effort to generate anything at all. But if you have the knowledge and understand how best to tell the story, it will come.

So, knowing all of that, let's ask ourselves that question again:

- Has there ever been a time when you've lost out on a piece of work that you were perfect for?

If you have - and most of us have - the chances are that you didn't lose the sale because you charge too much. And you didn't miss out because you haven't done any work in that particular industry...

The chances are that you **_lost out because you are not an_** **_authority_**. Or at least, you are not as much of an authority as the person who did get the gig.

We buy things from people we trust. If your prospects truly trust you, they will buy from you. But if you don't (yet) have the same level of trust as a rival, it's natural that you will miss out.

So where does trust come from? Typically, it comes from two places: Experience or Authority, so let's boil these down one by one.

Trust from Experience

This is the kind of trust you gain with others after knowing them or having worked with them for a while. Over time, people get a feel for you and what you are capable of. They understand your strengths and, crucially, they identify how your strengths can be of benefit to them.

Trust from experience can also be earned in other ways. For example, Implied trust - where a friend or a family member's trust of a person means you are more inclined to trust them too. Your brother or sister recommends a builder they used - that's trust from experience.

Age can also influence your trust - for as we age we are expected to accumulate more knowledge and to have learned more life lessons. And accolades such as awards, previous speaking engagements and books written can also make it easier to trust an individual or company.

Trust must be earned, but once you've earned the trust of your prospects, the door is open for you to sell to them - providing they have a need for what you offer.

Trust from Authority

Remember the doctor in the white coat I mentioned earlier? That white coat implies authority, which in turn builds trust. The doctor is in charge and has authority in the area of medicine, healthcare and generally making things better. Swap his white coat for a jumper and that immediate trust recedes, put it back on and it returns.

Now, your prospects want to buy from an authority. For those prospects, the discussion is not generally about price or having done identical work in the same industry. It is a question of trust, can they trust you over the alternatives they have? They need to see you as the authority, the person they can trust.

How to build authority

The million dollar question. And the good news is that building and establishing authority isn't actually all that difficult. All it takes is persistent effort. Small gains, established every day, over weeks, months and years.

Consistency is the key. There's no point establishing yourself as an authority over a period of weeks and months, then disappearing for a few months to concentrate on something else. You have to stay on it and stay at it, if not day in and day out then at least week in and week out.

That said, there are some things you can do to accelerate the process of establishing yourself as the authority, depending on how hard you want to work and how much time and money you want to invest.

For example, recording long-form YouTube videos can speed up the process. So too can creating comprehensive 'How To' guides as videos or as copy on your website that position you as the authority on your chosen subject.

Both of those options are fairly easy and very popular - but that popularity makes it problematic because it means that if you go down that route, you may struggle to make yourself stand out, to make yourself heard.

The best tactic to take here is to take a different route. If everyone in your field is doing one thing, try doing the opposite. If you're seeing an abundance of videos or how to guides, consider publishing a book. If I was to offer a single piece of advice to you on how to elevate your standing and make your voice heard to more people, it would be just that. Write a book. Write your book. Self-publish your expertise and watch the phone ring off the hook.

You might have broken out into a cold sweat at the thought of that, but self-publishing a book is not the same daunting task it once used to be. As someone who helps businesses self-publish their books and has successfully helped publish and launch thousands of titles, I can tell you it's now within the grasp of each and every one of us.

All it takes is the drive and patience to put your expertise to paper.

If you can commit the time to write your book, you're proving your authority. And if you can do that, you're elevating yourself above your competitors. Do that and you are absolutely winning.

Now as I said, the whole writing process is so much easier than it used to be, particularly if you take the fast-track option. What fast-track option is that, you may well cry? The one I'm about to explain to you in Chapter Three.

TELL ME A STORY

TELL ME YOUR STORY.

In recent years it has become very clear that the way to establish yourself as an expert or an authority is to write a book. The thinking is very simple. Write a book about whatever it is you do and you can become - pretty much overnight - a trusted authority on the subject.

Take Tim Ferriss for example. A prime example too. As you probably know, he wrote the book The 4-Hour Work Week, selling the world the dream of working less and living a better, richer life. Virtually nobody had heard of Tim Ferriss until he wrote that book, a book that has gone on to sell more than two million copies and been translated into 40 languages. Tim Ferriss blew up overnight and is now one of the most influential self-help writers of our generation, and much of that success can be traced back to the book.

Now I'm not saying that if you write a book, it will sell two million copies and make you filthy rich. You have more chance of selling two million copies of your book if you've written a book than if you haven't, of course, but selling millions isn't your priority here. Any book you write will be there to serve your business.

Look at it this way. If you wish to position yourself as an authority on your chosen subject, you need to effectively spread the word. You could potentially go down the face-to-face route, making yourself available for a series of one-to-one sessions online or in person, in which you outline why you are indeed the expert you claim to be.

But you think about the logistics of doing one-to-ones and you realise it will take you forever to reach the audience you want and possibly need to reach. So you upgrade and offer online workshops or seminars in which you sell yourself to a greater number of people in one session, and you wonder why you ever thought one-to-ones could work for you.

Only then you realise that if you wrote a book, you could have 10,000 copies of that book printed and sent out to potential clients and you'd be reaching numbers you could only previously dream of. At that point you realise that all the hard work is done in the writing process. Once the book is published, you simply wait for your clients to come to you, instead of going off chasing them every hour of every day. Consider it payback for the hard work you put in at the start of the process.

And here's another thought. Picture a scene. Close your eyes if it helps. You are standing alongside your competitors in a room, all smartly dressed and looking highly professional. You and your rivals are surrounded by four walls filled with potential customers and, you hope, long term clients. It's like shooting fish in a barrel. So how do you get their attention effectively? How do you make sure that when they leave that room, they remember you and not your competitors?

The American prohibition agent Elliot Ness had the right idea, explaining how you bring down the gangster businessman Al Capone. "You want to get Capone? Here's how you get him. He pulls a knife, you pull a gun. He sends one of yours to the hospital, you send one of his to the morgue! That's how you get Capone!"

Now I'm not suggesting you pull a gun on a room of clients, although they would definitely remember you if you did... But what I'm proposing here is just a little old-fashioned one-up-manship. While your competitors are left handing out just another business card, you pull out your book.

Your rivals gave them a telephone number. You gave them your expertise to take away and learn from. With that simple act, you are imparting your expertise, sharing your knowledge and towering above your competitors. And with that book, you have instantly established YOU as an expert in your industry.

And what's the CEO of a company going to pay more attention to; the 1,000th email of the month asking for 15 minutes of his or her precious time? Or the well-written book that lands with a thud on their desk? I can guarantee you that email is going straight to the junk files, but the book will sit on the desk and be lodged in their mind.

Now, it's said that we all have a book in us, but only a tiny percentage ever find the time to actually write the damn thing. The first barrier many would-be authors arrive at is the question of expertise. You may ask, how can I write a book on my chosen subject? Am I really an expert? And you will probably come to the conclusion that you are not, but you'd be wrong.

Nobody will tell you that you are an expert. There is no graduation ceremony, no expert qualification for being expert in anything. You just are an expert [although it does obviously help to have qualifications, proof of experience and maybe a few badges picked up along the way to confirm you know what you're talking about.] The problem most people encounter is thinking they don't know enough for it to make them an expert. This is nonsense.

They think and fear that there's always someone who knows more, therefore they cannot possibly be the expert. But that is nonsense too. There almost certainly is someone who knows more, that is true, but they may also be cowering behind the doubt that they are an expert, afraid to tell the world of their expertise for fear of being 'found out' in some way. And so, gripped by self-doubt, they never write their book and their expertise is kept hidden from the world forever. Which is sad and unnecessary, but it leaves the way wide open for you.

YOU are an expert and YOU choose how to position yourself.

Tell the world that you are a complete novice and that's how they'll see you.

Position yourself as an expert and the world will consider you an expert. [Note: being an expert doesn't necessarily mean you are the oracle, that you know everything there is to know about a subject. Note that we said an expert rather than the expert - there's a big, big difference. Being an expert means you know far more than the clients who need your services, and more than enough to do an exceptional job should those clients choose to pay for your services. To those people, you are an expert.]

The key to success in business is to be able to combine self-belief with positive action. Not so much self-belief that you become an insufferable arsehole, but just enough to understand the value of what you do and have confidence in your ability to deliver. And obviously you have to get off your backside and deliver - all the self-confidence in the world won't count for nada if you don't deliver what you say you will deliver. You will go from expert to fraud in the blink of an eye.

Now, I digress slightly, but we were always going to come back to the subject of your book. The book you want, need and deserve to write. To position yourself as an expert, you have to write your book, to commit your expertise to paper or, in this modern world, an electronic screen. As mentioned already, writing a book is the fast-track to establishing yourself as an expert.

But this brings us to another barrier many people fail to get over. When the subject of writing a book enters their head, they tell themselves that they shouldn't do that because they'd be giving away their secrets. This is a fair point if you write a book that details every last thing you know about your business, leaving no stone unturned and no subject uncovered. If you tell them every last thing you know, you've as good as given away the whole damn farm, and that is undeniably a bad move. [Trust me, dear reader. I'm not telling you every last thing I know about marketing your business in this book, just enough to pique your interest. I hope that what you read will establish me as a trusted authority in your eyes and that you will then be keen to find out more about what I can do to help you grow your business - in a fruitful, symbiotic, long-lasting working relationship that reaps rewards for both you and I.]

The trick with sharing your expertise is to tell them just enough to make them see that you know your business inside and out. Tell them enough to establish your authority. Tell them enough and they don't suddenly think they can do it all themselves and dispense with your services. Your aim is to get them to see you as the expert they trust so that they then want to use you to tap into that expertise. So that fear is also nonsense.

But that brings us to the next barrier many people encounter - the biggest and scariest of all. For a business person, a person engaged in the act of business on a daily basis, the thought of writing a book can bring them out in a cold sweat. Or a rash. Or both. Which is understandable.

As a businessman or businesswoman, you excel in business, not book writing. If you excelled in book writing, you'd be a book writer, and a bloody good one too with a holiday home on Lake Como and a gold Porsche. But you're not, so you haven't.

So this is where the doubts creep in again, where the barriers come up. But again, you are wrong. Let me explain why.

You may not be blessed with the writing skills required to write a book. Your grasp of grammar and punctuation may be exactly what the spell check was invented for. And as a successful businessperson, you may not even have the time to write a book in the first place. Those concerns are understandable. But they're also wrong. They are just excuses standing in the way.

You are not writing your Harry Potter or your Year In Provence here. This is not War And Peace or Schindler's List. You are writing the story of you and of what you do.

'Write what you know' is another well-worn cliché, but it's a cliché because it's true.

If you stick to your area of expertise - stick to what you know - your writing will flow more freely.

Now I'll come onto the act of writing your book in the next chapter - and I'll explain the simple techniques that make writing far easier than you ever imagined. But before we get to that point, I need to explain why I am telling you all of this. Let me get to the point.

I don't want to blow my own trumpet too long or too loud, but the fact of the matter is that over the last 10 years, my company, Elite Publishing, has helped more than 4,000 authors, entrepreneurs, and business professionals to write their book. We have helped them to publish, promote and profit from that book and by doing so, explode their income and their business. I'm too modest to bang that drum any louder, but let me bring in just three of those authors who have benefitted massively from writing their books and let them explain how their books helped their businesses grow.

"The first 20 books I sent out to potential clients got me three meetings," says Jane Hatton, author of *Even Break*. "Of those three, two of them went on to buy our services. These customers typically spend £10k with us a year, so two sales is a lifetime value of £100,000. The effort of writing the book and getting it published is well worth it when you consider the return on investment."

"Since Keris and I launched our first book with you some 18 months ago," says Matt Whitmore, co-author of *Fitter Food: A Lifelong Recipe*, "we have sold in excess of 10,000 copies worldwide and generated in excess of £200,000 worth of income from the book alone. This has helped position us as experts within our field and has led on to us presenting seminars all over the world, which again has generated even more sources of revenue. The book has been an unbelievable source of lead generation for our business. We did not fully understand when we set out on this adventure how much it would change our lives."

"I cannot recommend Bill and Elite Publishing enough," says Vicky Fraser, author of *Business For Super-heroes*. "Writing a book can open up a whole new world

of marketing and audience for your business and it can position you as an expert. It's an amazing lead generation tool."

Of course I'm blushing here, modest chap that I am. But my point wasn't to humble brag but simply to show how writing their book has helped position clients of mine as an authority in their field - and how writing yours could do the same thing for you.

Now I know what you're thinking here - it's what you're still thinking: I am no writer, Bill. I haven't written creatively since I was at school and even then I only did it because I had to. The thought of writing a full-size book still sends a shiver down my spine.

And that is still understandable. That's why so few people ever do get round to writing the book they have in them. But that's why the following chapter will lay out the process of writing your book in very simple terms and explain why it's well within your grasp.

CHAPTER FOUR

HOW TO WRITE YOUR BOOK

Unless you are a writer by trade, or you spend many of your working hours writing, you are not a writer. Statistically speaking, the vast majority of people are not writers. If you are not a writer, writing may not come easy to you. And if writing doesn't come easy to you, the thought of writing enough words to fill a book may well wake you up in the middle of the night.

Worry not, soon-to-be-published author, and believe me when I say writing your book will be far easier than you imagine.

Of those 4,000-plus titles Elite Publishing has published over the last decade or so, a large number were written by reluctant authors. They were written by people like you; people who doubted they had the time or the skills to be able to write a book.

The fact that those titles have generated in excess of £30 million and counting for those reluctant authors should prove why they were wrong to doubt their abilities.

And you are no different. What follows below is a very basic outline of how you can write your book quickly and efficiently. It only scratches the surface of our expertise when it comes to writing and publishing a book, but consider this a starting point on how you can get your creative wheels turning.

To keep things simple, we'll break it down into three key chunks...

1. Start Writing.

A typical book weighs in at between 40,000 and 80,000 words, though it can come in at much less than that. The book you're reading here is around 17,000 words from start to finish, and yours can be similar. There's really no point over writing or writing for the sake of filling pages. Remember the point made earlier about people being busy and impatient? Well that absolutely stands when it comes to writing books. But let's keep with 40,000 as a starting point.

Now 40,000 words is a daunting prospect, until you break it down into smaller, more manageable chunks. If you concentrate on writing 500 words a day, seven days a week, you will write your book in bang on 80 days, or less than three months. A book in three months is worth the sacrifice of time, is it not? But to do that, you have to be disciplined.

Set aside 45 minutes a day, ideally first thing in the morning when your mind is likely to be more creative, and get into the habit of making that 45 minutes a part of your daily routine. When you get in the habit of writing every day, you 'll establish a pattern and a chain. Five days, 10 days, 30 days and on - you'll establish a chain that you won't want to break, and before you know it, you'll have more than enough content to fill your book.

However, before you write a single word, you'll need to nail down this second point.

2. Choose Your Angle And K.I.S.S.

Write about what you know is perhaps the most important piece of advice anyone can ever give you before you begin writing your book. Pretending to be an authority on something you are not won't fool anyone. Neither will writing in a voice that is not yours. Much like assuming a 'telephone voice' when you speak on the phone to make you sound more intelligent or posh, you will sound entirely unnatural and very likely pretentious. Be yourself and let your real and true voice flow onto the page.

An equally important piece of advice is that you follow the acronym of K.I.S.S. - which as you'll no doubt already know stands for **_Keep. It. Simple. Stupid_** - or Sausage, if you'd prefer, because Stupid always feels unneccesarily confrontational. But that advice should be front of mind when you write anything at any point ever in your life, be it in or outside of business, post-it note, newsletter or PowerPoint presentation.

Few people have time to read content that is difficult to understand or follow. You may think that using big, clever words you find in the thesaurus elevate you to a higher level of writing and intelligence, but your readership will almost certainly disagree. They might even think you're an arse. Make something difficult for them to read and they will simply stop reading.

Your potential customers don't care about the jargon and technical nitty-gritty details that go on behind the scenes - unless you are selling technical stuff to technical people. Your potential customers are busy and they care about themselves and how you can help make their life easier. They want you to explain that to them quickly and easily, without them having to reach for the dictionary or the shotgun.

Tell your customers how you intend to help them in simple language. Avoid waffle. Keep your sentences short and sweet. And just to be clear...

KEEP. IT. SIMPLE. SAUSAGE.

Albert Einstein explained this better than I ever could: "If you can't explain it simply, you don't understand it well enough".

And if you don't understand it well enough to be able to explain it simply, why would anyone believe you are any kind of authority?

3. Establish A Structure

So you've set aside at least 45 minutes every day in which to write, and you are now aware that all the fancy highfalutin jargon bullshit has no place on any page you ever write, so you're almost ready. Next, you need to establish a structure for what you want to write.

Now, it's entirely possible that you could freestyle your way through writing a book, by which I mean start writing something - anything - and just see where it takes you. Eventually you'll hit the 40,000 word mark and you may well have a book on your hands. If so, well done, you lucked out.

There's a lot to be said for just writing - particularly if you find yourself struggling to get words down on the page. If it gets you through what some call writer's block, then absolutely do that.

But if you can, you should always look to establish a loose structure for your book - something that outlines what you want to say and where you want to say it, with some kind of sensible flow. Again, this is all very easy when you know how to do it - and this, in very basic terms, is how you'd do it.

Every book needs a beginning, a middle and an end, so let's take them in order.

The Beginning

How does your story start? Most likely, it doesn't start with you being born, coming out blinking into the big wide world and screaming the house down. That's how your story began, sure, but that's not likely to be of much use to a potential customer or client. Knowing what not to say is as important as knowing what to tell the world.

So your story here needs to start with you telling the world three things.

1. Who you - are in a professional sense.
2. What you do, professionally speaking.

And crucially...

3. How what you do can make your would-be customer's life better.

Just as it does with your website or landing page, your story in book form starts by you telling your reader how you can be of benefit to them if they call upon your services. By all means start with some colour - a breezy anecdote that helps set the scene - but keep it relevant to the point you are attempting to make. If it's not relevant, they may simply choose not to keep on reading.

In very simple terms, The Beginning should offer an overview, setting things up very nicely for The Middle.

The Middle

The good news with your Middle Section is that it shouldn't be difficult to structure or to write. Having offered an overview of the who, what, why and where in The Introduction, your middle section is where you add in the detail. This is where you share elements of your expertise in more detail, giving examples and case studies to add depth and insight and to establish your authority. All three parts of your book are crucial, and each section relies on the other two parts for it to work effectively, but the Middle is where all the big points are made and backed up with examples and proof. How you built this or that company up from zero to a multi-million pound multinational operation in the space of 18 months. The time you won local business leader of the year Eastern Region three years running. Your secret for improving productivity by 72% and still keeping your workforce happy and engaged in their jobs. Whatever it is that you do and however you've excelled at it, you should be including it here.

And with everything you write in The Middle, you should never lose sight of the need to be telling the reader why this matters to them and, most crucially of all, how they too can benefit. And all the while, the copy should remain easy to read, easy to understand and easy to remember. Typically, The Middle should take up the bulk of your book, though there are no set-in-stone rules where this is concerned. The only set-in-stone certainty is that after The Middle comes The End.

The End

Now The End is almost as crucial as The Beginning, in that it gives you the opportunity to remind the reader that they can benefit from what you do and should not pass up the opportunity to take the next step - be it by signing up to a newsletter, joining your unique online members club or by simply setting up a call at the very earliest opportunity to find out more. Everything you've written over the previous however many chapters is always building up to The End.

The good thing, for you, is that if your reader reaches The End, your Introduction and Middle section have worked as they should. By this point the reader wants to take the next step, otherwise why would they still be reading? So your job here is to get your message over the line and convert that interest into something more solid.

Remind them who you are, remind them what you do - and make it as easy as possible for them to follow up on the book by getting or staying in touch with you, be it via a phone number, email, website or any number of social media channels.

If you do that, you will have reached The End. And if you've reached The End, congratulations, you have written your first book - possibly your first Amazon best seller, and perhaps the first of many.

That book and any that follow on will help you establish yourself as an authority in your field - the authority figure I mentioned earlier, the expert people trust. It will elevate you above your competitors in an instant - or as long as it takes to print 10,000 copies of your book and set them to work. That book will ensure that your voice is heard above the noise.

Of course, the breakdown you've just read there is a very simplified overview of the whole process, but it's a process I follow with every book I've written and every time I work with a client or customer to get their expertise out of their head and onto the page. It's this very simple but proven process that has helped us publish more than

4,000 titles worldwide over the last decade, generating in excess of £30 million for people like you - people who know they have a book in them but maybe don't quite know how to get it onto the page.

And of course, writing the book is only the beginning. Once you have a book, you need to know how to most effectively use that book to open doors that might otherwise stay firmly shut. Used effectively, your book can help explode your business and elevate your name and reputation to a whole new audience. We'll come onto how we can make that happen in the next chapter.

CHAPTER FIVE

STAND WELL BACK - YOU'RE ABOUT TO EXPLODE

So you've written your book. You have 15,000, 20,000, 30,000, maybe 40,000-plus words down on page, hopefully written in as little as 80 days but written in whatever time it has taken you. Congratulations on joining the ranks of the published authors - you are in exalted and very excellent company.

But having written your book is not the end of the process. I mean, it can be if you want it to be. If all you want your book to be is proof that you had a book in you and that you actually got round to writing it, it's job done. Print it up, hand a few out to your nearest and dearest, put it on the shelf and pull it down whenever anyone comes to visit.

But if you're using your book properly, as it should be used, as more than just a vanity project, the book is just the beginning. Your book is the starting point, the tool you use to jump to bigger and better.

This is when the book starts to really work for you, to pay you back for the work you put in, getting it out of your head, onto the page and into print. If used correctly as a marketing tool or at the very least a calling card, your book could be the beginning of something very lucrative indeed.

Here's how things could unfold after your book has been finished, if you're being clever...

1. Publish Or Be Damned

Your book's title and cover art are nailed - and they read and look phenomenal. The book is then printed in whatever quantity you think you will need. Go small to start with is a good approach, but be ready to up the numbers when its reputation spreads. Nowadays you don't need to go searching/begging for a publisher to publish your book.

That was how it used to be, back in the dark days, back when the publishing world was controlled by a small but all-powerful cabal of king and queen-makers who decided what the world would read and when. Luckily, and happily, those days are now gone. Nowadays you can, should and will self-publish your book, and here's why.

A decade ago, 300,000 books were self published worldwide. Ten years later, that figure had risen to 15 million a year. And the numbers are continuing to climb. That remarkable rise confirms that you really should be writing and publishing your own book, because if you don't, your rivals almost certainly will. Put it another way: can you really afford to be left behind?

In as little as five working days, your books can be printed and distributed

In as little as five working days, the book you have worked so hard on will be printed and ready to go, a physical book in your hand, a dream finally realised.

And that's when things really should go into overdrive.

2. The Marketing Magic

So you have 100 copies of your book, although it's more likely to be 1,000 or more. The very least you should do at this point is to make some noise about your success as a published author. OK, you may not have had any tangible success as a published author yet, but simply becoming a published author is success in itself. [And by taking the next steps outlined below, the success should follow.]

Send the book out to your most valued customers and your most coveted clients. Offer a number of copies to the first 100 visitors to your website or the subscribers to your mailing list for free or at a discounted price. Spread the word on every social media channel you use that your expertise is now available as a book.

Then, break the contents of your book down into easy chunks and blog the very life out of it. Or drip feed your expertise onto Twitter, Facebook, Instagram, LinkedIn or wherever else you go to make noise in quick, bite-sized chunks. This is where the hard work you put in by writing the book will start to pay you back. The content you have can be resized a million different ways to give you expertise you can send out to your list. And you'll pause only to order more copies of the book to cope with the increasing demand.

If used wisely and used regularly, your book can be the most effective marketing tool imaginable. Your status as a published author will almost instantly elevate you to a higher level. You are now an authority on whatever subject your book has covered, and that book and your status will combine to boost your business and its bottom line as a result.

The next time you meet a potential new client, while all around you are offering limp business cards, leave them with a copy of your book. And wait for the call.

3. The Extra Special Sauce

What comes next depends on how hard you want to work your book. If you're happy dropping your expertise from the book into blogs or social media posts while handing out copies to customers or clients you're keen to attract, then the journey can end around about here. You have little more to do.

If, however, you want to aim even higher, this is where you shoot your book and your reputation into the stratosphere.

Now is the time to build [or rebuild] your website or a landing page around your book, creating a platform that allows you to use the book as the most potent marketing weapon in your arsenal.

You may already have a website of course - and as established earlier, if not, why not? - but you need to build the site around your book and use the book to drive your business on. Like a fisherman dangling a line into the lake with a juicy worm on the end, waiting for the big fish to bite, you should now use your book as bait to attract bigger fish in the business world.

Your book is a physical product containing your expertise that works almost magnetically. If people can see that the book exists, that they can get hold of a copy of it quickly and easily by just providing a few details, an email and a telephone number that adds them to your list, you are moving them a step closer to becoming a paying client, simply by marketing your expertise.

But of course it's more complicated than that, and what I call 'Special Sauce' really means the extra ingredients that go into marketing your business and driving it on to the next level of success. Done really well, your marketing should tick many, if not all of the boxes below.

1. Your Website And Landing Pages

The shop window to your world, this is where you will promote your book - and where you'll promote your business in general. As discussed earlier, your website [or landing pages] has to do more than just look pretty. It has to sell quickly and effectively your book and whatever else you are looking to sell. The language you use will need to be short, sweet and highly effective. You'll need to take out all the clutter, waffle and nonsense and get straight to the point, moving your potential customer/client from interested to signing on the dotted line as quickly and as efficiently as possible. And you'll need to make it work across all devices. This sounds easy, but it's not. Actually, it doesn't sound easy, because it's not. But it always follows a formula that gets your customer or client from A to B, Here to There or Start to Finish as quickly as possible.

2. A 52-week Email Marketing Campaign

Business is done by people trading with people. The bigger business is just the shell around people who ultimately want to do business with other people, with humans. To encourage someone to want to do business with you, you have to build a relationship, one built on trust. They have to like you - at least they have to like you enough to want to go into business with you. And the best way to build up a relationship, build trust and hopefully be liked by a customer/client is by making yourself a part of their life. The easiest way to do that is to have them as part of your list and offer them something they want. That new book that you wrote in 80 days - or better still, the contents of that book broken down into an email Masterclass - would work very nicely indeed.

Success is achieved by doing the small things over and over again. In this case that means staying in regular contact with your customer/client so that when they are ready to buy from you - and they will decide when this will be, not you - you are front of their mind.

Get them to sign up to a 52-week email where you offer the contents of your book. By offering this to them free, you are offering your expertise and keeping yourself at the front of the mind for when they are finally ready to do business. Little things done regularly, over and over and over again.

3. Social Media Marketing

The social media world can be a cesspit of humanity at its very worst, but it's really very good for reaching a wide market of potential customers and clients - if you use it properly. In terms of marketing your book, it can be highly effective.

The biggest problem with social media marketing is that it's oh so very easy to spend a lot of time and plenty of money doing exactly the wrong things. Because while there are vast numbers of potential clients sat waiting for you on Twitter, Instagram and Facebook, you may well find they are not in the mood for talking business. Often, when a person goes to any of those platforms, they go to be entertained - to look at a social feed filled with things that interest them - photos of glazed donuts or videos of ferrets who look like Tom Selleck, not so much to think about business.

The key thing with social media marketing is that you have to make it work for you. And by "work for you" I mean you have to get people off social media and onto your website and your landing page and onto your list, where you can control the conversation, build your relationship and sell them whatever it is that you're selling. The skill here, then, is knowing where to find your next customers and knowing how to move them from where you find them to where you want them to be - which is staring at your website or landing page and keying in their details to get a free copy of your book and sign up to your list. This isn't easy, but it has to be mastered to build your business effectively.

4. Online Videos

This one pretty much speaks for itself, but let me expand. The pen may well be mightier than the sword, but a video telling your clients how you can make their lives better is a weapon of mass destruction by comparison. People are busy, and some of the people you'll be aiming to reach will prefer to watch a video of you explaining what you're offering them rather than read screeds of text. That's why online videos can be particularly powerful in making sure your message is literally heard. If you're a bright, shiny, professional business, you'll benefit from having a series of bright, shiny, professional videos that you can use to sell yourself fast and effectively, ready to release to the world as often as you require.

The good news here is that anyone can make a polished video on their phone these days, so making a video has never been easier. But as always, knowing what to say - and what to leave out - is key to making an effective video.

5. Instant Google And Bing Traffic

As you'll have heard before, your website is your shop window. It's where people come to browse, some of them with a view to making a purchase - in this case, it's where they will come to buy your book but it's also where they'll visit to find out more about your business and how it can benefit them.

Some of the people who peer through your window are hoping to make a purchase of something specific. Some of them are open to making several purchases and perhaps signing up to a loyalty card so they can build up a relationship and do business long term. Sadly, some of them are just wanting to browse for a bit before buggering off to another shop down the road.

You can't easily control the quality of shoppers peering through your shop window to see what you're selling, but you can control the quantity. This is where search engines including Google and Bing can be your friend.

It breaks down into two camps here. The businesses that don't understand how to use search engines to their advantage, and the businesses that do. Those who don't understand search engines effectively have shops in back alleys - the type of place that passing trade never passes by. Those who understand how search engines work are located on Oxford Street - the footfall is frequent and heavy, and business is consequently booming.

As you'll discover in Point 6, search engines and SEO are not the be all and end all of business, despite what some people will tell you - usually people offering to do your SEO for you, at some outlandish price. That said, knowing just enough of the basics can help you to drive your website up search engines faster than your competitors. Understand the process - and it really is just a process - and you'll have an advantage over your competitors who don't have a clue what they're doing and operate on a wing and a prayer.

Knowing also how to read your results - what works and what doesn't - and then make changes accordingly also helps. To tweak and tweak and tweak again until you find the right formula can propel your business to places your rivals can't reach.

You don't need to be a digital marketing expert to make the online world work for you. You simply need to understand just enough to help you reach your audience faster and more effectively. Because as a wise man once bragged, knowledge is indeed power.

6. Optimised SEO

Ah yes, SEO, very much the follow on from No.5. If you can just master the dark arts of SEO, you'll unleash an almost biblical torrent of new clients desperate to (a) buy your book and (b) pay you for your services and expertise, right? Well, possibly, but not necessarily. SEO definitely has its place and it definitely pays to understand how basic search engine optimisation works - how choosing and using the right words within the right structure can help your website rank well in organic searches, as we touched upon above. But you shouldn't get too hung up on it and the chase for online customers.

Google is regularly moving the goalposts without warning, so one month you could find yourself with 85% of your website traffic coming via organic searches, but that can then drop to 10% the following month without you changing a thing.

In other words, SEO is hard to control, because you have very little control.

Knowing that is half the battle. Knowing that gives you back the time and the money you might otherwise spend chasing those google customers.

In your marketing, it's far more effective and beneficial to control the things you can actually control.

Also, people who come to you via a Google search aren't necessarily the type of customer you want. Yes, some of them might buy from you and some may stay with you for life - which is why it's absolutely worth building your website and understanding the basics of SEO to make it perform as well as it can.

But most people who arrive at your website likely don't already know you, and they're a long way from purchasing anything or committing to anything long term. Like I said earlier, building up strong, long term relationships in business takes time, which is why your list is so important to you. It contains the details of people already interested in your business, people you can build a relationship with over months and years so that once they are ready to make a purchase, at a time that suits them, you will be front of their mind.

Far better than to place too much faith in chasing face-less customers who may or may not happen upon your website. But like I said, give yourself an advantage over your rivals by at least understanding the basics of SEO, for it does clearly have its merits and so many people swear by it.

As ever, knowing where to focus your time, energy and money is absolutely crucial if you're to grow your business effectively.

7. The Power Of Remarketing

What is Remarketing? Put simply, it's a way to con-nect with people who've previously interacted with your website - people who were interested enough to visit your website but didn't complete a transaction of any kind. You know how you spend an afternoon looking at trainers/hats/guns, and the next day, every website you visit suddenly features ads trying to sell you trainers/hats/guns like the ones you were only looking at yesterday? It's that. The slightly unsettling sense that someone inside your computer is watch-ing you and peddling stuff you've been looking at?

Yeah, that.

It is slightly unsettling, but used in your business-es favour, remarketing can help position your ads in front of the people who've shown an interest but didn't quite get their chequebooks out. So that could be an ad for your book or an ad for your business, or it could be both. Keep putting the product in front of them and you'll increase awareness of whatever you're trying to sell. The more they see your product, the more likely they will be to bite.

Knowing how to remarket effectively is crucial, and it's something you have to get right.

8. Targeted Press Releases

You have written your book, so now you should do as the major book publishers do and issue a press release to tell the world it exists and how it can be ordered. If you write a book and tell no-one, what was the point?

A targeted press release can reap significant rewards if done correctly - both for your book and for building your relationship with your list. Knowing what to write, how to write it and how often to send it out are all important pieces in the big business marketing puzzle.

Get it wrong and you can turn potential clients against you forever.

Get it right and you'll build trust and find people who want to order your book and build a long-term relationship that works for them and for you. But you have to know how to get it right.

9. Showing Up On Social Media

As established higher up this list, using social media websites and platforms well is a tricky business. The noise on social media is deafening, the pace relentless, and it's very easy for your noise to get lost.

First off, you have to know where to position yourself - Twitter or Facebook or LinkedIn? - and what to say to maximise your chances of success. Remember, if you're on the wrong platform, preaching to a crowd of people who want to be entertained, not sold to, you're wasting your time and your energy.

And if you find the right platform with the right people but forget the golden rule: that it's not about you, it's all about how you can make their business and life better, then you're wasting even more of that time and energy.

You absolutely need to know what to say and where to say to help your business thrive.

10. Brilliant Blog And Vlog Posts

Finally, last and absolutely not least, the power of blogs and vlogs. Remember what I said earlier about positioning yourself as an expert - the whole reason you wrote the book you're going to write? Well blogs and vlogs are all part of that. And you remember when I mentioned the need to do the simple things over and over again, that repetition is the key to success? Well blogs and vlogs are all a part of that.

Likewise the need to build a relationship with your audience, to turn an interested viewer into a customer - and a customer into a long-term client. You have to connect directly and regularly with your audience using effective, insightful blog and vlog posts - if you want to maximise your chances of building your business. As ever, knowing what to say, how to say it and when to say it are all absolutely crucial.

Now 10's a nice number to run with there, but those 10 areas are just the starting point, merely a scratch on the surface of the things you could and really should be doing to maximise the potential of your book and leverage your expertise to take your business to new heights and greater markets. There is an 11th key tip, however, and it's perhaps the most crucial suggestion of all...

11. Outsource

Which brings us on to the final chapter of this particular book, and the one that could change your business and your life for the better, should you choose to turn the page...

CHAPTER SIX

HOW TO CHANGE YOUR BUSINESS - AND LIFE - FOR THE BETTER

There's no point in sugar-coating the truth: all of the above elements I mentioned take time and money to achieve. If you write a book, even using the fast-track process I've laid out in Chapter Four, it will take time and dedication to complete. Most people will fail, because it isn't easy. It's often out of your comfort zone and there's always something else you could be doing.

If you get to the end, having written your 20,000, 30,000, 40,000-plus words, you may understand the need to then take the next step and market the very life out of that book to help establish you as an authority in whatever line of business you are in. But again, that isn't easy. Much of it will be out of your comfort zone and there's always something else you could be doing.

Now, the more observant readers amongst you can see where this is going.

'Outsource', said Rule 11, and you'll probably remember me mentioning earlier that my own company, Elite Publishing Academy, has helped more than 4,000 authors, entrepreneurs, and business professionals to write their book, publish, promote and profit from that book and explode their income and their business. That number will have increased since I wrote these words.

But the point is, we have a proven track record, having helped so many people down the last decade.

Now, we'd be only too pleased to help you too.

We are all incredibly busy in the modern world, juggling balls and spinning plates day and night, five, six and sometimes sadly seven days a week. We understand completely that writing a book - your book - is yet another thing to add to a never ending To-do list.

However, we're confident in thinking that if you've reached this part of the book and are still reading, it's because you understand that this is something you really have to make time to do if you're going to propel your reputation and your business to the next level.

You recognise that writing a book is the quickest, most effective way to make your voice and message heard above the noise of a very crowded marketplace.

And this is where Elite Sales Generator comes in, because *we can help with any and every step of the content, publishing and marketing process*.

If all you require is our expertise to help you self-publish the book you write or have already written, we can help with that.

If you require assistance from the very Beginning to The End of your book, which can include help with structuring, tone of voice and even ghost writing, we can help with that too.

If you also want help in marketing the book effectively afterwards, via emails, your website, blogs or vlogs, social media channels, professional video marketing, professional content marketing, direct mail campaigns, optimised SEO, SEM, high-end web design and highly effective pay-per-click advertising, we can help with all of that and more.

If you require something in between and would prefer to pick and choose which options you need more assistance with, we can definitely help with that too.

Elite Sales Generator is an expert in helping people like you progress from aspiring author with a book in them somewhere, to fully published author with a book to their name and the world at their feet. Our expertise is extremely effective and proven time and again with clients at various levels and across numerous industries.

We can help give your book the push it needs to finally get it over the line, or we can help you start from scratch and be with you every step of the way.

By this point in the book, further words are largely redundant. By this advanced stage, you'll have made up your mind if writing a book is for you or not.

All that's left to say and do at this point is to thank you for taking the time to read this far, wish you all the very best in your business and drop my details off should you wish to carry on the conversation.

When you're ready to talk, please don't hesitate to drop me a line at *elitesalesgenerator.com/free-trial* and we'll get the ball rolling.

Thanks again and I will see you on the free trial.

Lightning Source UK Ltd.
Milton Keynes UK
UKHW041419260522
403568UK00002B/540